# WHAT IS ARTIFICIAL INTELLIGENCE?

Cody Crane

**Children's Press®**
An imprint of Scholastic Inc.

Thank you to our expert content consultant:
CJ Adams
Product Manager, Google AI Research

and our educational consultant:
Jackie Fego
Science Liaison
C.V. Starr Intermediate School
Brewster, NY



Library of Congress Cataloging-in-Publication Data available

ISBN 978-1-5461-7821-7 (library binding) | ISBN 978-1-5461-7822-4 (paperback) |
ISBN 978-1-5461-7824-8 (ebook)

10 9 8 7 6 5 4 3 2 26 27 28 29 30

Printed in China 62
First edition, 2026

Design by Kathleen Petelinsek
Series produced by Spooky Cheetah Press

# Find the Truth!

**Everything** you are about to read is true ***except*** for one of the sentences on this page.

Which one is **TRUE**?

**TRUE or FALSE** One advantage of AI is that it never makes mistakes.

**TRUE or FALSE** Cooling the computers that run AI programs uses up a lot of water.

**Find the answers in this book.**

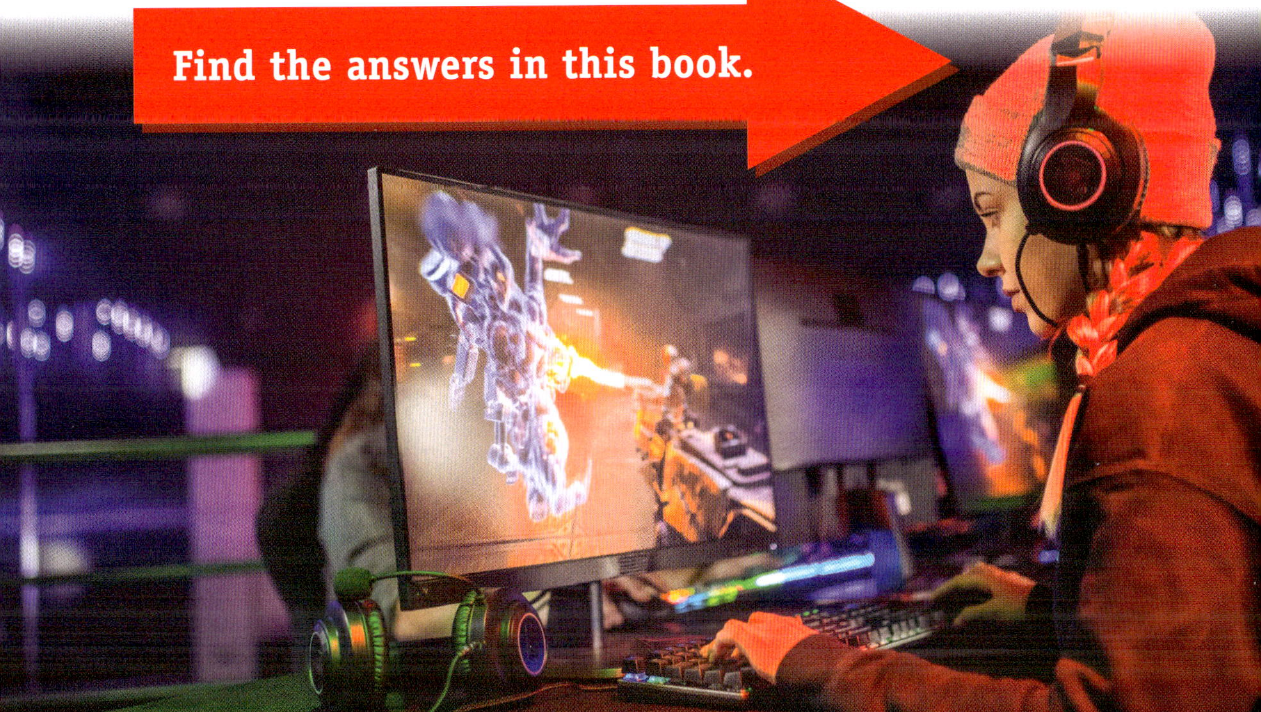

# What's in This Book?



Facial recognition tools use AI.

AI is used in space exploration.



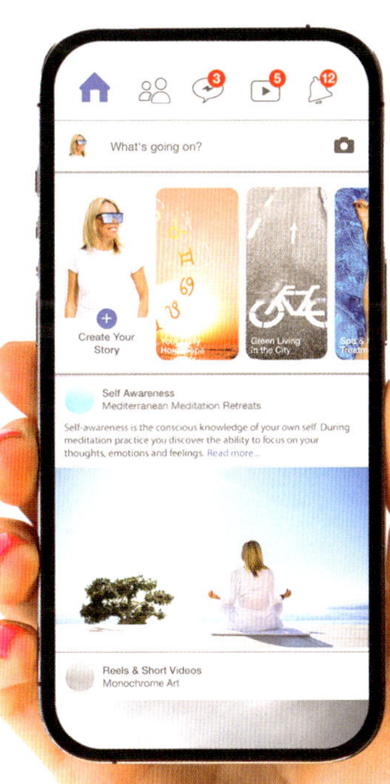


AI helps an app decide what you will see next in your feed.

Many cars have AI features—such as parking assistance and self-driving.

## INTRODUCTION

Television, airplanes, the internet. These are all inventions that changed people's lives in BIG ways. **Artificial intelligence**, or AI, promises to do the same. AI gives computers the ability to **perform tasks** usually only people can do. It allows **machines to learn** so they can do things like **understand language**, **solve problems**, and **make decisions**.

AI is not technology of the future. **It is here today.** Phones unlock using AI that scans your face. Some **cars** use AI to drive around without human drivers. **Social media** sites use AI to predict what content you might like. And those are just a few examples. People continue to find more and more uses for AI. Many think it will **transform** how we **learn**, **work**, and **play**.

John McCarthy was a professor at Dartmouth College in New Hampshire. He first used the term *artificial intelligence* in 1955.

This is ENIAC—the first electronic general-purpose computer.

CHAPTER

1

# The Rise of Thinking Machines

The first digital computers were created in the 1940s. They were used to solve complex math problems. From the beginning, scientists wondered if these machines could do more. In the 1950s, scientists began designing the first AI computer programs. One could play checkers against a human opponent. Another simulated a rat trying to find its way through a maze. But it would take decades of research to create more advanced AI.

## The Turing Test

AI does not actually think like a human. The best it can do is mimic, or copy, human intelligence. In 1950, scientist Alan Turing created a test to measure how well an AI could do this. Imagine texting with a person and with an AI. You ask both of them questions. Based on their answers, you have to decide who is the human and who is the machine. If you cannot tell the difference, then the AI passed the Turing test. Whether any AI has been able to pass the Turing test is being debated. Certainly some have come very close.

**Alan Turing (1912–1954) was a pioneer in computing and artificial intelligence.**

# What Are Algorithms?

A program tells a computer how to complete a specific task. To do this, the program follows a set of instructions called an **algorithm**. In regular computer programs, algorithms are like a recipe you would follow to bake a cake. If you follow the exact steps of the recipe, you should create the same dish each time. AI's algorithms are different. Instead of following a set of steps, they can process huge amounts of data (another word for *information*), identify patterns in it, and then use that understanding to come up with new solutions in the future. Each time they are given new data, AI algorithms can use it to improve how they perform a task. That is what allows AI to learn, and why the results AI gives us might be different each time.

Regular computer programs use algorithms the way people use recipes. AI algorithms are able to create new, more efficient outcomes.

## Human vs. Machine

For a long time, AI technology mainly remained the stuff of science fiction. Then the company IBM created a powerful chess-playing computer called Deep Blue. In 1996, the AI-powered computer played against world chess champion Garry Kasparov and lost. The next year, Deep Blue beat Kasparov in a rematch. This success was followed in 2011 by another IBM-made AI named Watson. It beat two *Jeopardy!* quiz show champions on live TV.

**After their second match, Kasparov was angry that the computer had beaten him. He accused it of cheating!**

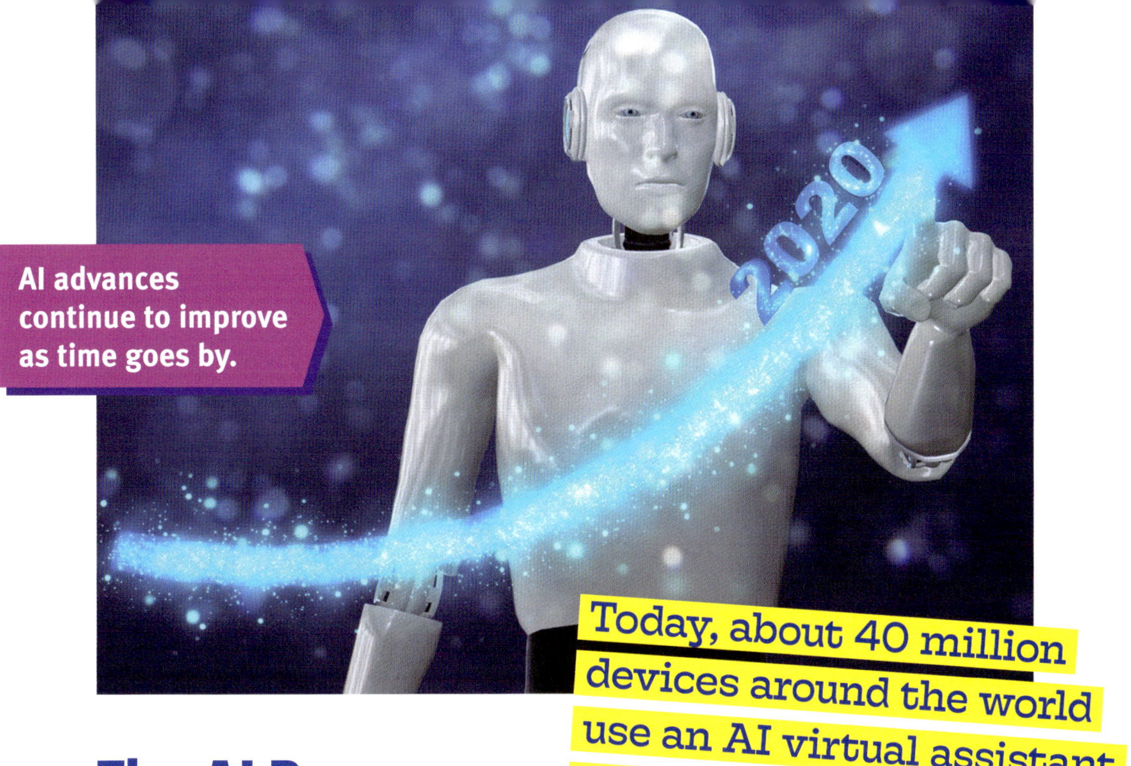


AI advances continue to improve as time goes by.

Today, about 40 million devices around the world use an AI virtual assistant like Alexa.

## The AI Boom

In the 2000s, AI technology began advancing at a rapid pace. Scientists were no longer creating game-playing AI just to show what the technology could do. They started making AI that could perform real everyday tasks. They began adding it to all sorts of technology, including phones, cars, and vacuum cleaners. This marked the beginning of the AI boom. We are still in the middle of this period of rapid growth in AI technology.

In 2016, Sony Music created the first AI-generated pop song.
AI can be used to create different types of art.

CHAPTER

2

# Types of AI

AI has come a long way since it was first dreamed up several decades ago. Today, there are many types of AI, each used for a different purpose. These AI **models** use a variety of methods to learn. Most AI help people by analyzing information to draw conclusions. Some go a step further, taking what they learn to create songs, books, art, and more. Let's explore the main types of AI models, how they are created, and how they are used.

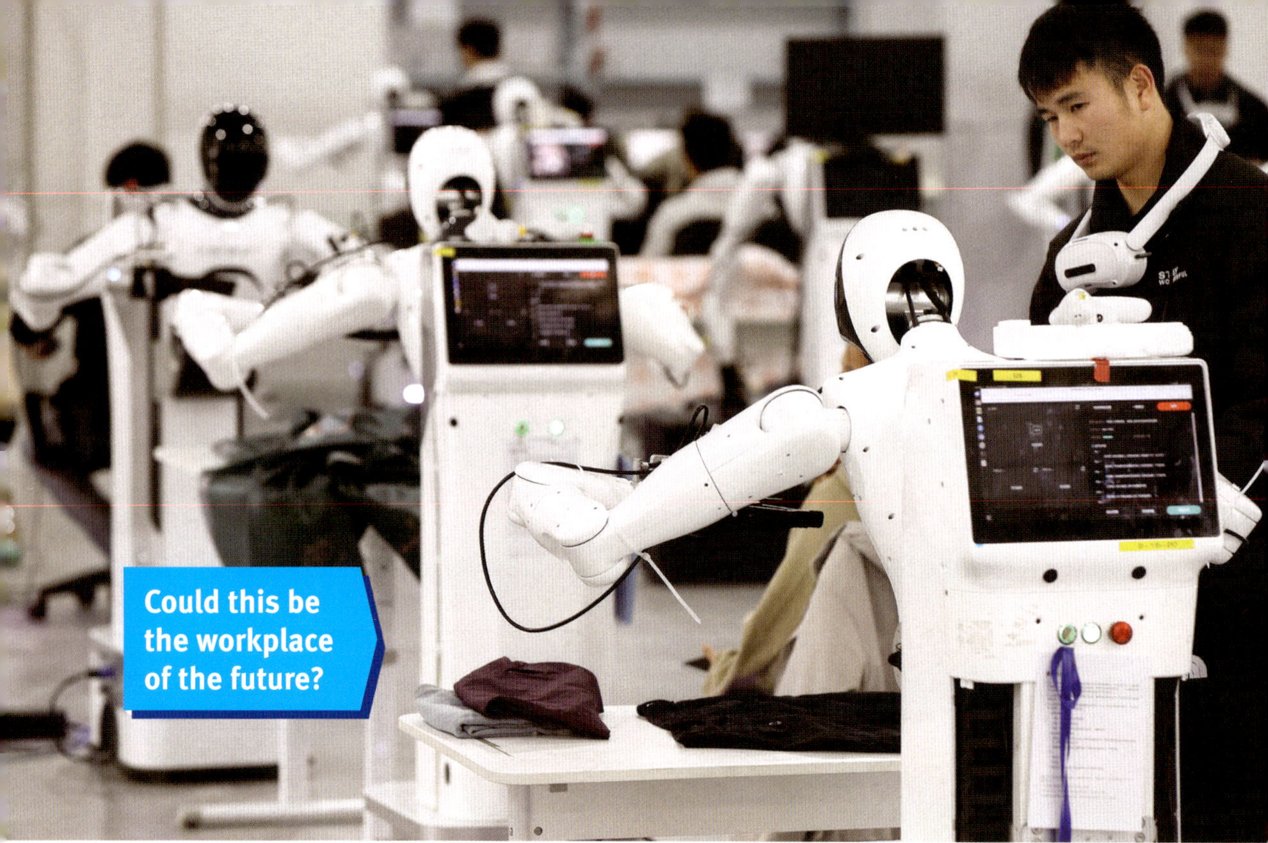


## It Starts with Data

All AI models need to be trained to perform tasks. This can be done by giving the AI a **dataset**. A dataset is a huge collection of information. An example might be all the books ever written. The AI analyzes the dataset. It is taught to look for information, make connections, and draw conclusions.

## Machine Learning

How would you teach a baby what a dog is? You could show them a picture of a dog and say "Dog." Over time, the baby would learn to recognize a dog. One type of AI called machine learning works in a similar way. It is given examples, like images of dogs and humans. The images are labeled so the AI knows which are pups and which are people. Then the model analyzes the relationship between the images and labels. Eventually, it learns to tell the difference between the two.

Email programs use machine learning to sort out unwanted junk mail so you do not have to read it.

Studying with flash cards is similar to machine learning.

## Deep Learning

Deep learning is another type of AI. It uses a system called a neural network. A neural network processes information in layers. Each layer learns to look for certain features. This gets more complex as information moves from one layer to another. For example, deep learning is used for recognizing faces. Its first layer might learn to spot shapes that look like faces. The second layer looks at the distance between facial features. A final layer identifies who the face belongs to.

A transformer is a type of neural network that was introduced in 2017. It revolutionized how AI understands and generates language.

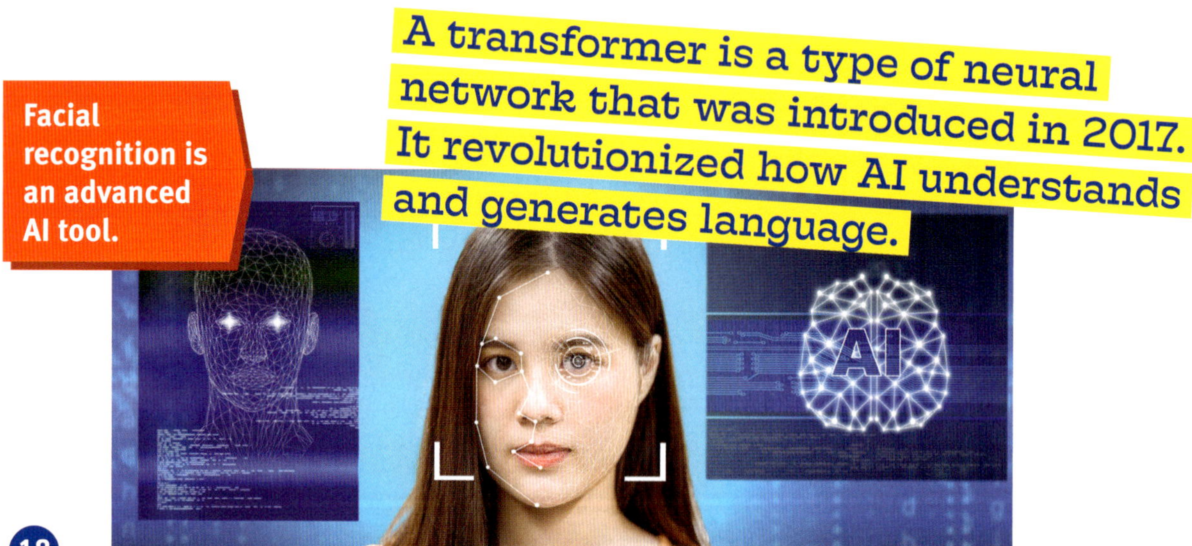


Facial recognition is an advanced AI tool.

# AI-Powered Bots

What if you took an AI model out of a computer and put it into a robot? Then the AI could interact with the world around it. It could learn to identify and pick up objects or navigate around obstacles. In fact, many robots today rely on AI. It allows them to be **autonomous**. That means they work on their own, without humans controlling them. AI-powered robots inspect and put together items in factories. They zip around warehouses, finding and carrying packages. And they plant, water, and pick produce on farms.

Can you spot the little blue robot moving this shelf around?

The online retailer Amazon has more than 750,000 AI-powered robots working in its warehouses to help sort, pack, and ship customers' orders.

There are more than 7,000 languages spoken in the world. The number of languages AI can recognize is increasing rapidly.

## Large Language Model

Imagine you want to learn a new language. You memorize vocabulary words. You study how the words form sentences. Then you practice having conversations. A large language model is a type of AI that can learn to understand human languages too. Virtual assistants, like Siri and Alexa, use this type of AI to understand and respond to your questions. So do apps or websites that predict what you will type next or that correct your spelling.

# Generative AI

Generative AI, or GenAI for short, is a recent innovation. These types of AI are trained to look for patterns in datasets, like written texts, images, or music. But they do not stop there. GenAI models apply what they learn to generate, or create, something new. One of the most famous examples of GenAI are chatbots, like ChatGPT or DeepSeek. They mimic human conversation. They can predict which words are most likely to go together. This allows them to create actual speech.

ChatGPT gained more than one million users in the first five days of its release in 2022.

You can interact with chatbots by typing, talking, or even having a video call.

The BIG Truth

# Should Chatbots Help

GenAI tools, like ChatGPT, can do many tasks quickly. For example, give them a **prompt**, like "Write an essay about how magnets work," and the AI will do just that in a few seconds! This worries some teachers, who fear students might use AI for schoolwork. Let's hear why some students use AI and why others avoid it. Then decide what you think!

GenAI tools can help us brainstorm ideas for a school project, like coming up with a list of science fair ideas.

Chatbots can answer questions anytime, even when teachers or parents are not available to help. They can also explain things in different ways until we understand them.

GenAI tools can make studying for exams easier. For example, we can ask a chatbot to create a set of sample questions that we can use to practice for a test.

Chatbots can help us gain new skills that will allow us to do better in school—like playing an instrument, writing code to program computers, and learning a new language.

**Yes. Chatbots are great help for schoolwork.**

# with Schoolwork?

Some tools can scan students' work to see if it was created by an AI. Like many new technologies, though, it is prone to making mistakes!

**No. Chatbots should not help with schoolwork.**

If we rely on chatbots too much, we will become lazy and miss out on learning things by ourselves. For example, if we ask GenAI to research a topic for us, we will never learn how to do it properly ourselves.

Chatbots might not always give us the right answers when we ask them a question.

Using chatbots too much might mean we spend less time talking to real people for help. And chatbots can't understand our feelings or know when we're struggling with something.

Using GenAI tools to do our schoolwork is the same as copying off a classmate. Even though GenAI content was created by a machine, passing it off as our own is still **plagiarism**.

AI has been used in video games in different ways since the 1950s.

AI is often used in video games to create characters that behave like real human players.

CHAPTER

3

# AI in Action

Most people do not even realize it, but AI is all around us. It is in our homes, in our communities, and on the internet. Families use AI to plan vacations, workers use it to write emails, and scientists use it to program computers. Even kids like you are using AI to surf the web, play video games, and more! And its uses only continue to grow. Let's look at some real-life examples of AI at work.

## On the Web

Most search engines use AI to summarize topics you search for. Shopping sites use AI to do the same for product reviews. AI tailors what ads and content you see on websites and apps based on your online activity. For example, video sites like Netflix use AI to suggest shows based on others you have watched. Many websites also use AI chatbots to answer customer questions. These AI tools aim to customize and improve users' experiences online.

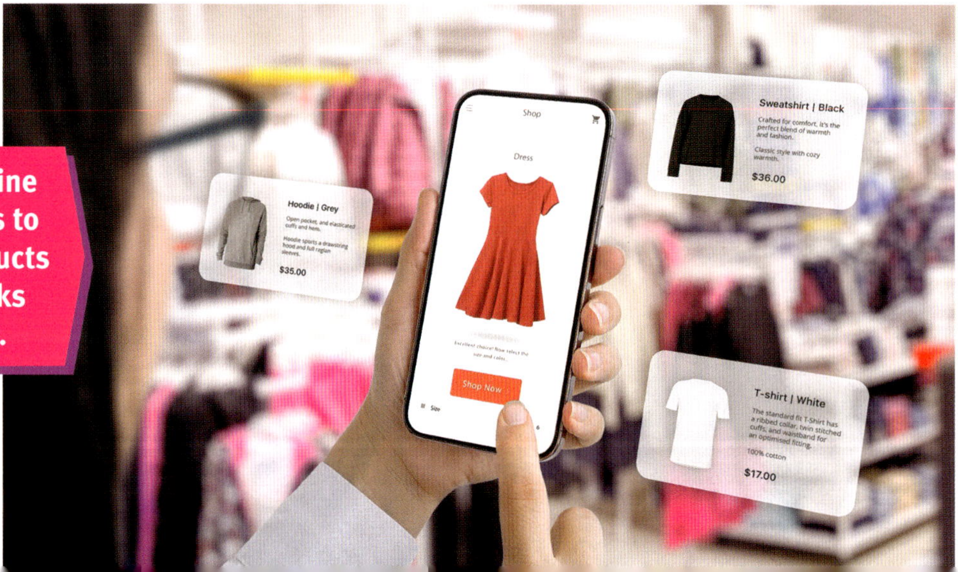

**AI enables online shopping sites to offer you products the seller thinks you might like.**

Machine learning is used to predict weather.

If you check the weather on a phone or another device, it is likely an AI forecast.

## Rain or Shine?

Should you grab an umbrella before heading out the door? AI can give you the answer. AI processes huge amounts of recent data from weather stations and satellites and uses that information to make highly accurate forecasts in a matter of minutes. And it can make these predictions weeks in advance. That can provide life-saving information to people ahead of extreme weather, like hurricanes or heat waves.

## Assisting Doctors

AI can be taught to examine medical tests, like X-rays, to look for problems. It can then give doctors advice to help them make a faster and more accurate diagnosis. AI can also review a patient's medical history and look for patterns. This can help doctors come up with the best way to keep the person healthy. AI can also screen databases of potential medicines to find new treatments for different diseases.

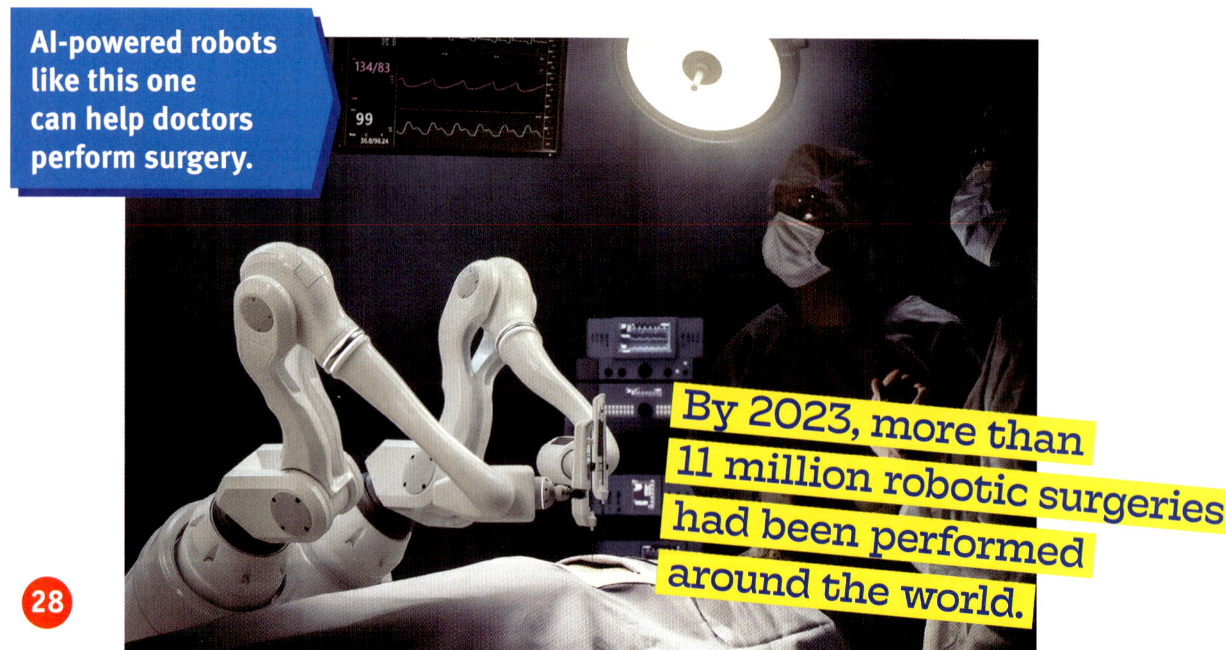


AI-powered robots like this one can help doctors perform surgery.

By 2023, more than 11 million robotic surgeries had been performed around the world.

## Fighting Crime

Say a security camera records a person committing a crime. Before the police can arrest the suspect, they have to figure out who it is. AI trained to recognize individuals' faces can help police more easily identify the person. AI is also helping in spotting crime online. Banks use AI to monitor people's accounts. The tools look for unusual purchases or transactions.

**Unusual activity can mean someone is trying to steal from a person's bank account.**

Police also use facial recognition tools to search for people who have gone missing.

## Smart Homes

From the speaker by your bed, your virtual assistant tells you it is time to wake up. You pass your robotic vacuum as you head to the bathroom. The lights in your kitchen dim automatically. Then your home security system alerts you that your friend has arrived to walk to school. This is not a scene in some futuristic movie. These are all real AI-powered devices that exist in millions of people's homes today.

### Timeline of Advances in AI

**1952**
Arthur Samuel develops the first computer program that can learn to play a game (checkers) by itself.

**1966**
Joseph Weizenbaum creates ELIZA, the first program that mimics human conversation.

**1998**
Cynthia Breazeal creates Kismet, a robot that can react to people's emotions.

**2004**
NASA lands the *Spirit* and *Opportunity* rovers on Mars. They navigate the planet's surface on their own using AI.

**2006**
Social media and video streaming sites start using AI to determine what content to show users.

## On the Road

Here's something to think about the next time you are in a car. Not all vehicles sharing the road are being driven by humans. Some might be using AI to drive themselves! They have sensors and cameras to detect traffic lights, road markers, and other vehicles. That is not the only way AI is changing how we get around. Some of the apps we use to get directions also use AI to choose the fastest routes for users.

**2011**
**Computer company Apple releases the first iPhone with Siri, the first AI voice assistant that can respond to questions and commands.**

**2022**
**The company OpenAI releases ChatGPT—introducing generative AI to the public.**

**2024**
**Google adds AI-generated summaries of topics to users' searches.**

**2025**
**DeepSeek, a chatbot created by a company in China, is released to the public. It may use fewer resources than similar AI tools.**

"Deepfakes" are images, videos, or audio files of people created by AI that look and sound like they are real.

This Google data center is in the Netherlands, a country in Europe. It houses the equipment needed to run computer programs and AI.

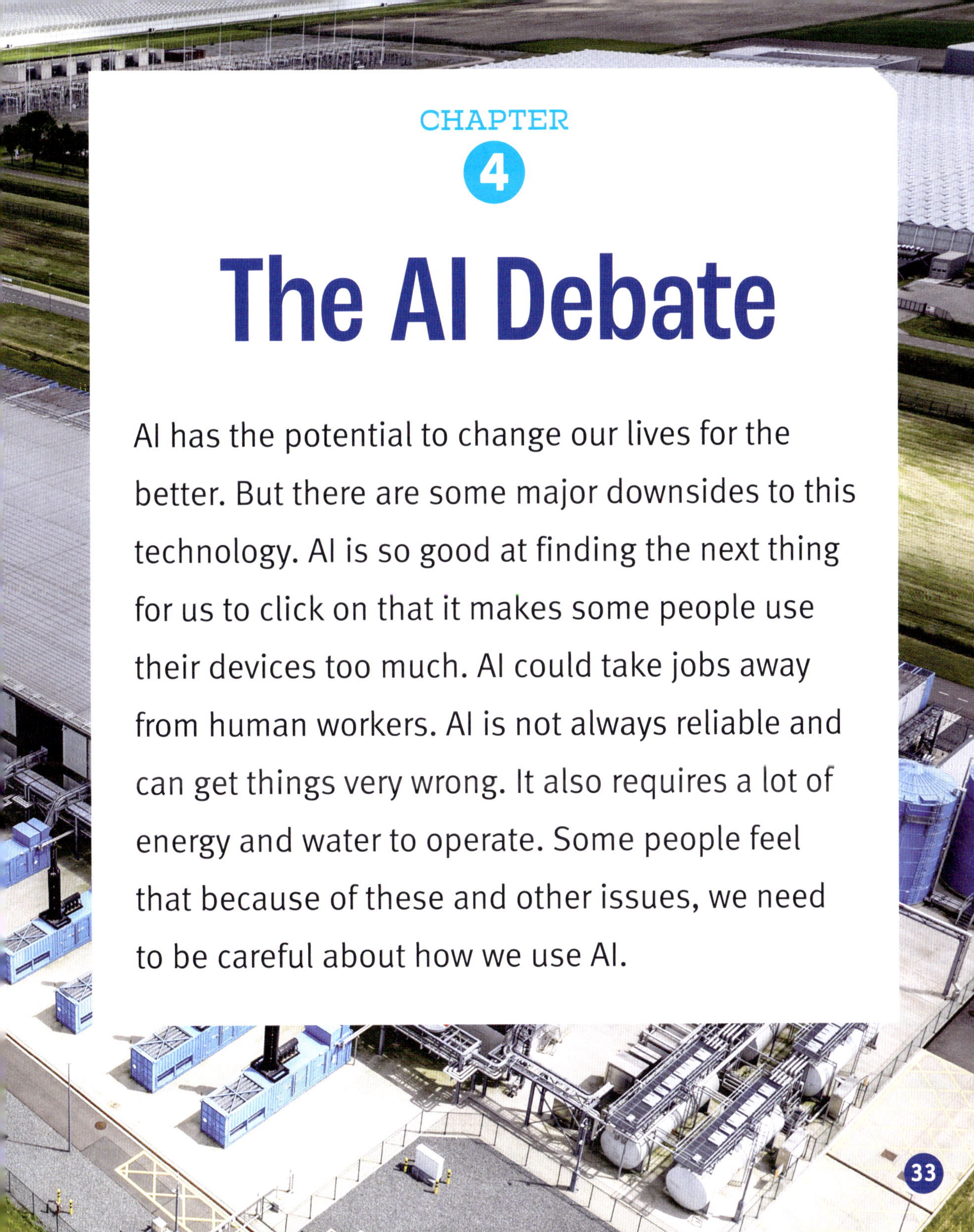

CHAPTER
4

# The AI Debate

AI has the potential to change our lives for the better. But there are some major downsides to this technology. AI is so good at finding the next thing for us to click on that it makes some people use their devices too much. AI could take jobs away from human workers. AI is not always reliable and can get things very wrong. It also requires a lot of energy and water to operate. Some people feel that because of these and other issues, we need to be careful about how we use AI.

This is *The Starry Night*, a painting by Vincent van Gogh.

This is an AI-generated copy of *The Starry Night*.

## Stolen Property?

Many companies have come under fire for how they train their GenAI models. The data they use to feed these tools are real examples of art, books, and other materials created by humans. These works are often protected by **copyright**. This rule says only a work's creator can decide how it is used. Artists and writers argue that their works are being used to train AI without permission—and therefore illegally.

# Replaced at Work

Artists and writers have something else to worry about from AI: being out of a job. Movie studios are turning to AI to review scripts and create realistic backgrounds and visuals for films. News sites are using AI instead of human reporters to write articles. Other jobs are in trouble, as well. Many people fear AI will replace more and more human workers going forward.

In 2023, TV and movie screenwriters went on strike, in part to protest the use of AI to do their jobs.

Many businesses already use AI for data analysis, writing emails, and more.

## Fake Out

One troubling feature of GenAI is that it sometimes states false information as fact. This is called a hallucination. It can happen when an AI does not have enough information or is confused by a prompt. People can also use AI to make fake voices, images, videos, or news articles that seem real. This can spread dangerous misinformation online by tricking people into believing things that are not true.

A well-known hallucination happened when Google's search AI told a user they could use glue to keep cheese from falling off pizza!

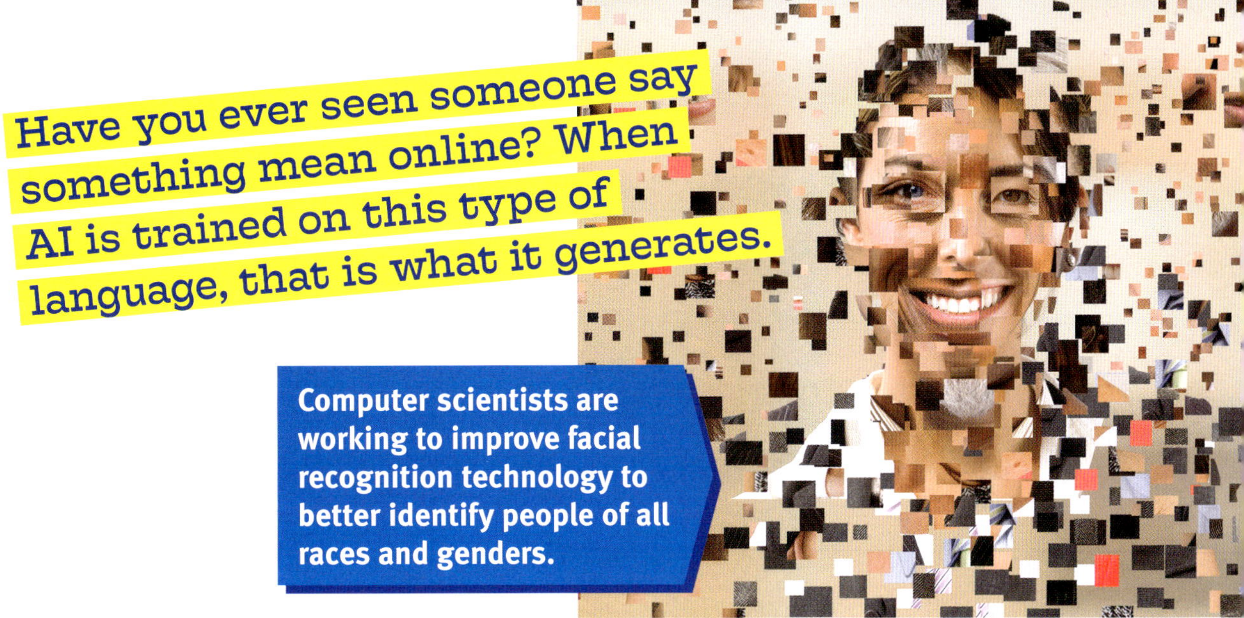


Computer scientists are working to improve facial recognition technology to better identify people of all races and genders.

## Negative Stereotypes

Because AI learns from information created by humans, it can often contain human **bias**. An AI's responses might include negative ideas about certain groups of people because of their race or gender. Bias in AI can also happen when the data used to train these tools lacks diversity. For example, most facial recognition AI was trained using images mainly of white men. As a result, it often makes mistakes when trying to identify people of color, especially women.

# Environmental Impact

AI models are complex. They require warehouses filled with computers to be trained and used. Powering all those computers requires lots of electricity. Most of that comes from burning fossil fuels like coal, oil, and natural gas. And that creates pollution that worsens **climate change**. As computers run AI programs, they get hot. A lot of water is needed to keep the machines from overheating. Some people think this is wasting a valuable resource.

Every 5 to 50 prompts typed into ChatGPT use up about one bottle of water.

This is what it looks like inside a data center.

After reading this book, are you more excited or more concerned about the future of AI?

## The Future of AI

AI is getting smarter every day. It could make our lives better in many ways. But these advances come with risks. AI has grown so powerful so quickly that people are now realizing we need laws regulating its use. Governments around the world are working on these types of policies. They include rules about what data can be used to train AI models and ways to reduce misinformation and bias. The goal is to make sure AI tools are safe, fair, and trustworthy.

# Animal Chat

A sperm whale swims through the ocean. It makes a series of rapid clicks and squeaks. The other whales in its group respond with their own calls. Scientists have long wondered what these sounds mean. It is possible the whales are speaking to one another. And AI might be able to translate what they are saying!

For 13 years, a group of scientists recorded the sounds made by 400 sperm whales in the Caribbean Sea. Then they used AI to look for patterns in the recordings. The model identified 156 unique sounds. Scientists think these may be the sperm whales' alphabet—the building blocks of language. Researchers are working on figuring out how this alphabet fits together to possibly form words and sentences like human speech.

Other scientists have used similar AI tools to decode elephants' rumbles. They discovered that individual animals in a herd have different names. Dogs have had their barks analyzed by AI too. The technology could tell a playful "Woof!" from an angry one.

RUMBLE!
RUMBLE!

With the help of AI, we are learning to better understand the animals that share our planet. It is possible that someday we could even talk to them one-on-one!

# Using AI Wisely

AI is a powerful tool, so you need to make sure to use it responsibly. Here are some smart tips for how to use this technology safely and wisely.

## Always check with a trusted grown-up before you download any AI apps.

An adult can make sure that these tools are kid-friendly and safe for you to use.

## Never share your personal information with an AI chatbot.

AI tries to learn more about you so it can give more personalized answers. But information you do not want to be shared with others—like your full name, address, and phone number—should be kept private and not shared with an AI either.

Remember, AI analyzes your online searches, the websites you visit, and what you click on.

It uses this information to target you with ads for products and content you may like. This might make you overuse your device.

Avoid using AI tools, which require a lot of energy and water, when you could use a simpler method.

For example, do not use AI to solve a math problem when you could use a pencil and paper or calculator to find the answer yourself.

Do not use AI to create or share fake images, videos, or other content that could be harmful or misleading.

This could spread misinformation—and get you in trouble.

# True Statistics*

- **Percentage of people in the United States who use digital AI assistants, like Siri:** 46%
- **Number of driverless taxis operated in three U.S. cities by the company Waymo in 2024:** 700
- **The highest price ever paid for an AI artwork:** $1,084,800 USD (It was a painting of scientist Alan Turing created by a robot called Ai-Da.)
- **Number of jobs worldwide that could be replaced by AI by 2030:** 300 million
- **The amount of money spent on AI tools worldwide in 2024:** $184 billion USD
- **The amount of data used to train AI models:** Recent large language models were trained with more than 10 trillion words from all sorts of different sources (equal to about 100 million books).

* As of 2024

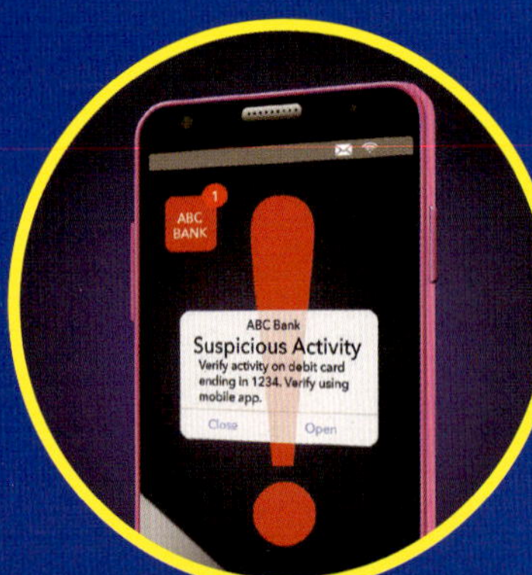


## Did you find the truth?

**FALSE** One advantage of AI is that it never makes mistakes.

**TRUE** Cooling the computers that run AI programs uses up a lot of water.

# Resources

## Other books in this series:

## You can also look at:

Dugal, Matthieu. *Welcome to AI: What Is Artificial Intelligence and How Will It Change Our Lives?* London: Wide Eyed Editions, 2024.

Hutchinson, Sam. *Artificial Intelligence: Activity Book*. New York: Racehorse, 2024.

Johnson, Brian David. *What You Need to Know About AI*. London: Wren & Rook, 2024.

Oxlade, Chris. *Computer Science for Curious Kids*. London: Acturus, 2023.

Richardson, Michael Lee. *The Extraordinary Life of Alan Turing*. London: Puffin, 2020.

# Glossary

**algorithm** (AL-guh-rith-uhm) the set of instructions a computer follows to complete a task

**artificial intelligence** (ahr-tuh-FISH-uhl in-TEL-i-juhns) the science of making computers do things that previously needed human intelligence, such as understanding language

**autonomous** (aw-TAH-nuh-muhs) the ability to make choices and decisions and to act independently

**bias** (BYE-uhs) a tendency to favor or oppose a particular group or person; prejudice

**climate change** (KLYE-mit CHAYNJ) global warming and other changes in the weather and weather patterns that are happening because of human activity

**copyright** (KAH-pee-rite) the legal right to control the use of something created, such as a song or book

**dataset** (DAY-tuh-set) a collection of related pieces of information that can be searched and manipulated using a computer

**models** (MAH-duhlz) AI systems that are trained to recognize patterns and make predictions

**plagiarism** (PLAY-juh-riz-uhm) stealing the ideas or words of another and presenting them as your own

**prompt** (PRAHMPT) input or instructions given to AI

# Index

Page numbers in **bold** indicate illustrations.

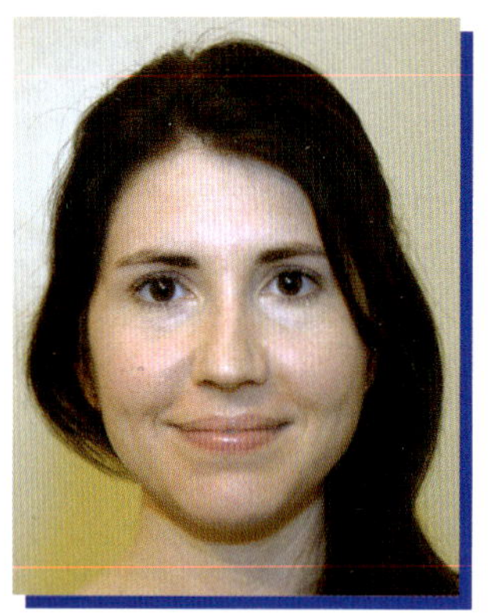

## About the Author

Cody Crane is an award-winning nonfiction children's writer. Her favorite subjects to write about are science and art. She plans to read this book with her ten-year-old son.

**Photos ©:** cover: Yuichiro Chino/Getty Images; 3: zeljkosantrac/Getty Images; 5 top: NASA/JPL-Caltech; 8–9: Science Source; 10: Aclosund Historic/Alamy Images; 11: StockPlanets/Getty Images; 12: George Widman/AP Images; 14–15: BlackJack3D/Getty Images; 16: Tang Yanjun/China News Service/VCG/Getty Images; 17: Jose Luis Pelaez/Getty Images; 19: Bav Media/Shutterstock; 21: portishead1/Getty Images; 24–25: zeljkosantrac/Getty Images; 27: Traimak_Ivan/Getty Images; 28: gorodenkoff/Getty Images; 30 left: IBM; 30 center left: Christoph Keller/Alamy Images; 30 center: Sam Ogden/Science Source; 30 center right: NASA/JPL-Caltech; 32–33: Robin Utrecht/Shutterstock; 34 left: Universal History Archive/Shutterstock; 35: David Swanson/Bloomberg/Getty Images; 37: John M Lund Photography Inc/Getty Images; 38: Thomas Trutschel/Photothek/Getty Images; 40 bottom: Flashpop/Getty Images; 42 left: Deepak Sethi/Getty Images; 42 right: Ole_CNX/Getty Images; 43 top left: Daviles/Getty Images.

All other photos © Shutterstock.